BENJAMIN LAW is a writer whose work spans non-fiction, screenplays, journalism, stage plays, documentaries and essays. His debut play *Torch the Place* was staged by Melbourne Theatre Company and will be restaged by Queensland Theatre in 2026. He is the bestselling author of *The Family Law*, which was shortlisted for Book of the Year at the Australian Book Industry Awards and adapted into three seasons of the award-winning SBS TV series of the same name, for which Benjamin was creator, associate producer and screenwriter. He is also the author of *Gaysia: Adventures in the Queer East,* the *Quarterly Essay Moral Panic 101* and editor of *Growing Up Queer in Australia*. As a screenwriter, Benjamin won an Australian Writers' Guild Award Award for his work on the SBS drama *New Gold Mountain*, and worked as co-executive producer, co-creator and co-writer of the Netflix series *Wellmania* (2023).

DYING: A MEMOIR

An adaptation by **Benjamin Law**
Based on the book by **Cory Taylor**

CURRENCY PRESS
The performing arts publisher

MELBOURNE THEATRE COMPANY

CURRENT THEATRE SERIES

First published in 2025
by Currency Press Pty Ltd,
Gadigal Land, Suite 310, 46–56 Kippax Street, Surry Hills, NSW 2010, Australia
enquiries@currency.com.au
www.currency.com.au

in association with Melbourne Theatre Company

Typeset by Brighton Gray for Currency Press.
Printed by Fineline Print + Copy Services, Revesby, NSW.
Cover shows Genevieve Morris; photo by Jo Duck.
Cover design by Sarah Ridgway-Cross.

Currency Press acknowledges the Traditional Owners of the Country on which we live and work. We pay our respects to all Aboriginal and Torres Strait Islander Elders, past and present.

A catalogue record for this book is available from the National Library of Australia

Contents

Director Jean Tong, Writer Benjamin Law and Genevieve Morris in rehearsal (Photo: Emily Doyle)

Director Jean Tong in rehearsal (Photo: Sarah Walker)

Writer's Note

I can't remember how Cory Taylor and I became friends. What I do remember is she was finishing her screenwriting PhD as I was starting mine, that we trusted each other enough to read each other's works in progress, and that she was a regular customer at Avid Reader—the indie book shop where I worked—and had excellent taste in books. For a while, my youngest sister and her eldest son also dated, so our families overlapped. Also, this was Brisbane. Writers just know each other there.

Naturally, I felt pretty lousy that I didn't know Cory was sick for such a long time, until I read *Dying: A Memoir* and discovered she had been keeping her diagnosis from so many people, including her family. In her final weeks, Cory's publishers at Text Publishing fast-tracked the memoir's publication, furiously proofreading and typesetting the pages as Cory submitted them, ensuring she could hold a copy of the book before she died. In her final weeks, we all gathered at Avid Reader for the launch, communing with Cory via Skype. We were relieved that she had held in there long enough to launch the book, and griefstricken to know what was coming. Shortly after, Cory died.

One of Cory's editors at Text Publishing, Caro Cooper, will tell anyone who will listen that Cory is one of the Australian authors everyone must read. If Cory had started publishing novels at twenty-five instead of her fifties, Caro says, her volume of work would have put her in the league of Winton or Garner. I agree. For those who knew Cory, there is an ongoing ache that so few people know her work, despite the fact *Dying: A Memoir* was longlisted for an Australian Book Industry Award, shortlisted for the Stella Prize, endorsed by Julian Barnes, Margaret Drabble and Hilary Mantel, embraced by the *New York Times* and chosen by Barack Obama chose as one of his Top Ten Books of 2017.

To some extent, I've written this adaptation of *Dying: A Memoir* with a sense of responsibility to my late friend's legacy. However, dutifully faithful tributes don't tend to make for compelling theatre. It has been a long process of untangling my feelings of fealty to Cory and her book, to ensure the story earns its place on the stage.

Cory and I would sometimes talk about the work of David Hare, who once said, 'The great mystery of adaptation is that true fidelity can only be achieved through lavish promiscuity.' So here, with the guidance and encouragement of Melbourne Theatre Company—especially director Jean Tong, Head of New Work Jennifer Medway, and Artistic Director Anne-Louise Sarks—is an adaptation that has pulled the form and shape of Cory's memoir apart. In doing so, I feel it has paradoxically aligned itself with the spirit and mission statement of the book: to pull us from the sorrowful loneliness of dying, to a place where we're in conversation with dying as a reality—together, as a community.

Benjamin Law, 2025

Dying: A Memoir was first performed by Melbourne Theatre Company at Arts Centre Melbourne, Fairfax Studio, on the lands of the Wurundjeri Woi Wurrung people of the Kulin Nation, on 25 October 2025, with the following cast and creatives:

CORY	Genevieve Morris

Director, Jean Tong
Set and Costume Designer, James Lew
Lighting Designer, Rachel Lee
Composer and Sound Designer, Darius Kedros
Associate Composer and Sound Designer, Todd J. Bennett
Stage Manager, Oriana Papa
Assistant Stage Manager, Lucie Sutherland

NEXTSTAGE

Commissioned and developed through Melbourne Theatre Company's NEXT STAGE Writers' Program, with the support of our Playwrights Giving Circle.

Melbourne Theatre Company acknowledges the Boon Wurrung and Wurundjeri Woi Wurrung peoples of the Kulin Nation, the Traditional Custodians of the land on which we work, create and gather. We pay our respects to all First Nations people, their Elders past and present, and their enduring connections to Country, knowledge, and stories. As a Company we remain committed to the invitation of the Uluru Statement from the Heart and its call for voice, truth and treaty.

Genevieve Morris and Director Jean Tong in rehearsal (Photo: Sarah Walker)

Genevieve Morris in rehearsal (Photo: Sarah Walker)

CHARACTERS

CORY TAYLOR

NOTES

(*Brackets and italics*) denotes the actor talking directly—as brief asides—to an audience member. These are suggestions only. Feel free to improvise at these moments to maximise irony, comedy and intimacy with the audience.

Bold indicates when the actor switches to another character.

This playtext went to press before the end of rehearsals and may differ from the play as performed.

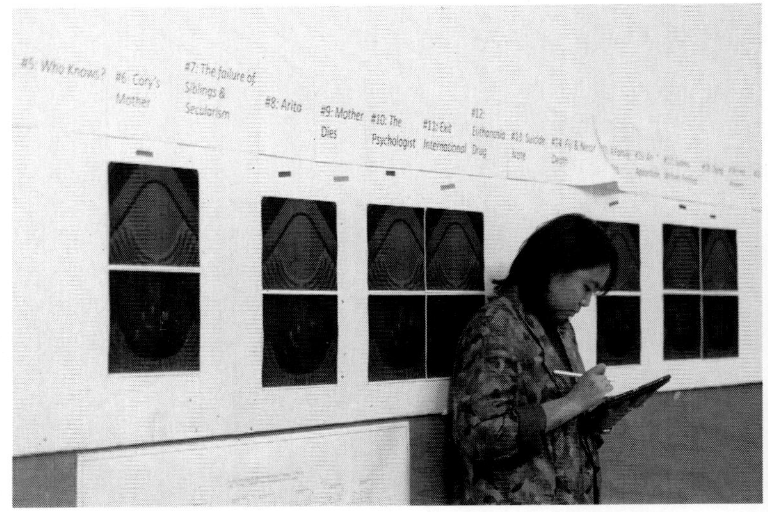

Lighting Designer Rachel Lee in rehearsal (Photo: Sarah Walker)

Set and Costume Designer James Lew in rehearsal (Photo: Sarah Walker)

PROLOGUE

Audio announcement, and then from an unexpected spot in the theatre:

ACTOR: Hello! Up here. To your left. Not that left. LEFT. Yep, that's it.

As the ACTOR *clumsily walks through the entirety of a row in the audience:*

(*Yep, legs out of the way, drinks out of the way—you do have a drink? Trust me, you're going to need it.*)

(*Bit of theatre etiquette, 'scuse me, coming through. Actually, I can't remember, was it crotch to the face or back to the…*)

Hi there. My name is [ACTOR's name] and tonight I'll be performing as Cory Taylor. Now, you might be wondering who Cory Taylor was.

Well, she was a writer, who wrote screenplays, novels and children's books. She was also a mother, a wife, a daughter, a sibling. And like most of us, she didn't really think too much about death, until she had to.

Now, before we start, I'm going to need all of you to pull your phones out and turn them off. And I mean *off.*

ACTOR *goes to an audience member and gestures for the phone.*

Is it off?

May I see?

(*IF YES, EITHER:*

That's just airplane mode, does this *look* like an airplane to you?

OR:

Good job! Setting an example for the rest of row [number].

IF NO:

That's fine, you can say no, it's private property.

We shouldn't touch strangers' phones; petri dishes for germs.)

Oh, another thing! This play is about dying. *No prizes for guessing who.*

[*To audience member*] (*It's a one-woman show.*)

I know. *Dying.* Bit of a downer.

Nobody likes stories about death, right?

[*To another audience member*] (*Well, you bought a ticket to this play/RSVP'd to opening night. You tell me.*)

But seriously: we have such a collective aversion to death! Why is that? Is it because we're scared? In denial? Alone?

Yes, this play will hurt. You might cry.

But you'll also laugh.

[*To another audience member*] (*Oh, you'll laugh.*)

You may get so overcome by emotion that you'll need to exit abruptly. Not because the play is bad—

[*To another audience member*] (*It's frankly a masterpiece; the acting is a triumph ...*)

No, it's because all of us have—or will—experience loss. And all of us will die.

It's the one thing every single person on the planet has in common.

(*You're really regretting coming to this, aren't you?*)

But seriously, if the people in your aisle need to get some air, be kind.

Offer a tissue if you have it. Actually, do you have one?

(*IF YES:*

Oh thank you, I might need that later.

IF NO:

No worries.

Produces tissue.

I prepared this one earlier!)

Yes, dying is confronting, but guess what? In this theatre, right now, we're in this together.

Are you ready?

[*To another audience member*] (*You don't look ready.*)

Either way, here we go.

The ACTOR *steps onto the stage.*

'*Dying: A Memoir*.'

Suddenly the theatre is plunged into darkness, whether the audience is ready or not.

A DIAGNOSIS

Lights come up on CORY TAYLOR, *late fifties/early sixties, holding a numbered ticket: 83.*

She sits in the waiting room in a nondescript medical setting. We hear sterile noises—trolley wheels, squeaky shoes, air-conditioning, a filtered water dispenser gurgling.

Numbers are called out: '76' ... '77' ... '78' ...

CORY: It's a lonely business, dying.

If cancer teaches you one thing, it's that we're dying in droves, all the time.

If you saw us all, out on the street, you'd never know it. But we're everywhere.

Death seems to be this unspeakable thing.

Even here there's this monstrous silence.

But how does that help anyone?

Beat.

It's melanoma, if you're wondering.

Biopsy on a mole. Back of the right knee. Comes back: cancer.

Just before my fiftieth birthday.

(*Quite a shitty birthday present.*)

It's 2005 and the first time I hear the word 'cancer' in a doctor's setting.

The doctor is very … informative.

The doctor speaks like a slow, robotic automaton:

DOCTOR: Well, Cory. We have the results. As I suspected, the excised cutaneous lesion demonstrates malignancy, with a Breslow thickness of two-point-two millimetres, one mitosis, no ulceration, with reasonable risk of recurrence even after surgical excision.

CORY *looks at the audience. She may mouth: 'What the fuck?'*

You have cancer.

CORY: Oh.

DOCTOR: **Level Four.**

CORY: [*with alarm*] Stage Four?

DOCTOR: ***Level* Four. Common mistake. The Clark level system is frequently conflated with clinical staging nomenclature, though these metrics are neither analogous nor interchangeable.**

After another baffled pause.

CORY: Right … So, what happens from here, doctor? What should I expect?

DOCTOR: **Melanoma is notoriously unpredictable in terms of prognosis, development and pace. Things can move very slowly, then all of a sudden …**

Pause.

… very fast.

CORY: So what does that mean? Do I have—what? Five years? Five months?

DOCTOR: **Oh. Well, it's a complex situation. Entirely dependent on myriad factors: tumour biology; disease distribution; host-related variables. And intercurrent complications: neutropenic sepsis; thromboembolic phenomena; treatment-induced organ toxicities …**

Another baffled pause.

Honestly, it's hard to tell.

CORY: I'm taken aback, but I also can't help thinking of how … *ordinary* this moment is.

Getting a cancer diagnosis isn't like the movies … where some handsome man in a white coat says you've got a certain number of months to live, then the string section starts …

Cinematic strings swell. CORY *reacts: 'Yeah, like that.'*

… and your hair artfully falls out from the chemo and you cry with cinematic dignity in the shower.

Strings abruptly stop.

No. Outside I hear construction. A school bell rings. I have errands to run after this.

It's almost offensive, but life continues.

SPLIT SECONDS FROM DEATH

CORY: I've already nearly died once.

[*To audience member*] (*I promise it's a good story.*)

It's about a decade ago.

Here's what I remember:

I step out of my parked car. A split second later:

A speeding sedan. Going too fast. Through a red light.

The sedan hits three other vehicles; jack-knifes into mine!

I stand there, staring, in complete shock.

A bystander sees the whole thing; comes rushing over:

BYSTANDER: Jesus Christ, you were a split second from losing yer fucken legs!

CORY: The driver's young; only a teenager. He's shaken-up but emerges unhurt.

Says he's sorry: brakes failed; couldn't stop.

He looks ashen. I must too.

One split-second. Just a few millimetres.

That was the difference between me keeping or losing my leg.

CORY *smiles for the twist.*

My *right* leg … which has a mole on it.

A mole already over-exposed to UV radiation.

The mole that will soon turn into melanoma.

The melanoma now so intent on killing me.

[*To same audience member*] (*Told you it was a good story.*)

What might've happened if I'd lost that leg? If I'd been a second slower stepping out of the car?

I'd be legless. But I mightn't be dying now.

We're all just split-seconds—millimetres—away from death, all the time.

A DIAGNOSIS (*CONTINUED*)

CORY: But now, my doctor can't even say the word 'dying'.
I *am* dying though, aren't I, doctor?

DOCTOR: Oh. Well. My job is to keep you alive. [*Coughs*] But I do have a brochure you can read.

CORY: It's extraordinary. Doctors deal with the reality of death every day, but the last thing they want to do is even mention the word.

DOCTOR: You are also eligible to claim six hour-long counselling sessions, courtesy of the Cancer Council. And it's all free.

The doctor raises his eyebrows.

CORY: I think he's excited?
(*Very unnerving.*)
I'm ambivalent about the counselling sessions, but he writes up the psych referral, just in case. The only thing he needs for it is a legitimate condition.
Uh, how about 'dying'?

DOCTOR: Condition: Adjustment disorder.

CORY: [*laughing*] You're making that up!
(*He isn't.*)
As he writes the referral, I'm suddenly seized by thoughts of a slow, painful death.
Doctor, just so you know … I'm not a believer in the virtues of stoic suffering.
For the record, I'm up for any and all forms of pain relief.
Or, better still, just shoot me.

DOCTOR: I'll make a note.

CORY *smiles but chugs down a glass of water, now visibly anxious.*

CORY: Some of you already know what it's like to get a diagnosis like this.
Your mind slows down from shock, then you're seized with endless questions.
What happens now?
How long have I got?
Who do I tell?

(*No-one.*)
(*Everyone?*)

WHO KNOWS?

CORY: You might assume I would've made a big announcement.

But I don't want to needlessly panic anyone.

And as the days—then weeks, then *months*—pass by, nothing really changes, health-wise.

I feel … the same?

Intellectually, I know I'm staring down my mortality, but it doesn't seem like I'm … [dying]

(*Well, you know.*)

So the only person I tell about my diagnosis is my husband, Shin, who comes with me to all the appointments and tests.

I don't tell my kids.

I know what you're thinking, but why should I upend everything for them? Nat's an artist; Dan's a musician. They're in their twenties. They're young. They're happy.

They're living their lives.

(*They're living.*)

The last thing I want is for them to be consumed by my illness …

When you have kids, things change. Suddenly, your only job is to protect them, no matter what—even into adulthood.

I still remember walking my sons to school when Dan—my youngest, then in Year Four—turned to me at the school crossing and said, 'You can go now, Mum.'

'Bye, Mum.'

'Bye.'

Laughs.

I already knew that would be out last little mum-and-son walk to school. And that as time went over, there'd be only more and more signs that I was unnecessary.

And I can't help but feel that if I have to deteriorate, that's okay—as long as my children thrive.

So life goes on. Life is busy. And life is demanding. Especially considering:

CORY'S MOTHER

Crucifixes slowly descend into the space, along with images of the Virgin Mary and the saints. Lit church candles, possibly. We're getting Catholic.

CORY: My mother is dying too.

Dementia, if you're wondering. Diagnosis: cortical atrophy. Just before her sevenieth birthday.

She's barely recognisable now.

Can't take care of herself; neither can we.

So several months ago, we chose the only option available and placed her in a nursing home.

Finally, a large and gruesome crucifix—an obscene bloodied rendition of Jesus of being crucified—descends.

It's a Catholic institution.

[*To audience member*] (*As you can see.*)

We were told, 'It's a very good facility.'

She scoffs.

Jesus Christ.

[*To the crucifix*] 'Sorry.'

If this is a good facility, what constitutes a bad one?

Some of you have been in these places.

You know the smells, the sounds. How it tests your willpower to even walk through the door.

Soon after my diagnosis, I gather myself and walk in, only to see my mother …

CORY *turns away and winces.*

… clutching onto a bathroom basin with all her meagre strength as a young exasperated nurse wipes her arse.

The look in my mother's eyes as she sees me is like an animal in pain.

We insist on prolonging life, but is it worth it, if you feel irreversibly trapped and miserable?

None of us expect to die in a place like this, do we?

No, we fool ourselves into thinking:

We'll be rich and have a private nurse. Or we'll die in our sleep at home, when we're ready. Or we'll start a commune.

CORY *laughs.*

Ha. With what money? In what world?

It's likely most of us will end up in aged care.

Yet we're in denial. I am too.

Can't afford to be any longer though, can I?

As she sits to clips her mother's nails:

I sit with her to clip her nails. She's not altogether there.

Mum? It's me. Cory. Your youngest daughter.

MOTHER: Can't remember.

CORY: Cory Taylor. Youngest of three.

MOTHER: Cory was my grandmother's name …

CORY: I know. You named me after her.

MOTHER: Granny's dead now; Mum's gone too. Now it's my turn, I guess.

But darling, you're young.

You don't have to worry about that for a very long time …

CORY: I don't have the heart to tell her we're both dying. Is it wrong to think that I'd rather kill myself than go out like my mum?

It's ironic, but Mum was the one who introduced me to the debate around 'voluntary euthanasia'—as they called it in the eighties.

I assumed our discussions were hypothetical. Academic.

Now I wonder: was she actually asking me for help? For when the time came?

What did she ultimately want?

Can't have been … *this*.

THE FAILURE OF SIBLINGS & SECULARISM

CORY: The longer I take care of Mum, the more desperate I am to leave the country.

Shin is Japanese, and several years ago, we bought a house in the town of Arita—the birthplace of Japanese porcelain. The plan was to split our time between there and Brisbane.

But as Mum gets worse, I tell my sister …

I can't go to Japan now. What if Mum dies while we're away?

SISTER: **Cory, come on. Worst case scenario? Mum *does* die.**

We cremate her, then we figure out what she would have wanted later.

CORY: But we know so little about what Mum wants.

We try to ask, but it's clearly too late.

She barely knows who she is, let alone that she's dying.

She'd told us she wanted her remains in Toowong Cemetery, her name on the same granite plinth as her parents and grandparents.

But other than that …

SISTER: **Okay! Process of elimination.**

What *wouldn't* Mum want?

Nothing fancy.

Nothing religious.

Nothing traditional.

Nothing …

A beat of gallows humour.

Suppose that's an option too: *Nothing.*

CORY: We laugh.

She encourages the audience to laugh—

WE LAUGH.

—then immediately stops laughing. Scoldingly:

We're terrible.

SISTER: **Alright, how about a party?**

CORY: Perfect! Mum loves a party.

SISTER: **And if the worst happens, Cory, we'll wait until you and Shin are back and throw a big one.**

You've been grieving her all these years anyway. Mum won't mind. It's not like she'll be going anywhere.

CORY: I'm still not entirely sure what constitutes a good death.

But I do know some people make the process better for the living.

My sister's one of them.

I still can't tell her about me though. Not yet.

But I *do* fly to Japan.

ARITA

In Japan.

CORY: My first visit to Japan was in 1982.

I was intoxicated by everything I saw. Cherry blossoms in Shirakawa. Hip bars in Yanaka. Snow falling on cedars from an onsen at Mount Aso.

In all of these places, I thought to myself, 'I could happily die here.'

Then Shin came along, and the deeper I fell in love with him, the more I fell for Japan.

Shin's a painter. We bought this place in Arita because the town is synonymous with porcelain. He likes the idea of painting on something permanent, rather than something that will die.

The river that runs through the town is layered with discarded blue-and-white porcelain shards—broken plates, cups and teapots—from artists long dead.

Shin and I go for walks in Arita, surrounded by beauty and nature.

He paints. I write. Or at least, I try. To be honest, I'm completely stuck on my new novel. I suspect it's the diagnosis, hanging over me like the Sword of Damocles.

(*Is this the last thing I'll write? Better make it count!*)

But … it doesn't matter. I'm alive. The world is alive. And hearing the river outside, I don't feel frustrated by writer's block.

I feel peace and calm, prepared for anything—

A phone rings and CORY *reacts, amused/appalled. Then:*

Oh wait. Hang on, that's *my* phone.

She picks it up.

Hello?

[*To audience member*] Hey sis. Any news on—

Pause.

When?

Pause.

How?

Pause.

Oh.

She lowers the phone.

MOTHER DIES

CORY: According to my sister, Mum only wanted to see our brother as she was dying.

He came to sit with her, keeping vigil, holding her hand.

He took control, charging ahead with a religious service at that hideous Catholic facility.

It all happened before I could even get home.

Our sister didn't attend, refusing to step foot in that place again.

Our brother held onto Mum's ashes.

My sister and I still wanted to throw a party, but then I came home and time passed, and passed, and passed …

Life continued.

Then we realised: it had been *a year* and we still hadn't done anything.

The three of us meet at a Chinese restaurant Mum loved.

I'm looking forward to seeing my sister.

To be honest, I've always been a little afraid of our brother.

Anything we say can set him off without explanation or logic.

I can't exactly say why communicating with him is so difficult.

I call my brother maybe twice a year—if that—to update him on Mum's health.

But now, that's not exactly needed.

At the restaurant, my sister brings up the idea of a party.

BROTHER: A party?! Our mother's dead; we're not waving her onto Fairstar the Fun Ship.

CORY: (*Fair point, well made.*)

BROTHER: Mum deserved better than that.

It's what *you* want, not what she would've wanted. You're just thinking about yourselves.

CORY: (*Maybe he's right. Maybe we are.*)

BROTHER: Now what are we eating? And don't say duck. Dirty, disgusting bird …

CORY: (*I don't point out that we were in a restaurant that specialises in duck.*)

SISTER: How about the scallops and snow peas with ginger?

BROTHER: Don't eat seafood. Hate ginger.

SISTER: Remind me: are you allergic or do you just not like the taste?

BROTHER: Does it matter?

SISTER: It matters if you don't want us to murder you from anaphylaxis.

Accidentally, I mean.

CORY: It's never a conversation with our brother, only an argument.

It's like we're combatants before we're siblings.

I try changing the mood: Mum loved the scallops, remember?

BROTHER: Well, Mum's not here now. And I *was* … while you were off gallivanting in Japan.

CORY: Well, I was actually in Japan struggling to write a novel while contemplating my own impending death.

(*I don't say that.*)

He's in a mood the entire night, stays as briefly as possible, doesn't even consider dessert.

Before he leaves, he unceremoniously fetches something from under his chair.

CORY *retrieves a plain plastic tub, spins it around and reveals the word 'Mum' on it.*

A whole life, and this is what we're all reduced to.

Don't worry; we'll be responsible. We'll do well by Mum.

The brother scoffs.

BROTHER: Whatever you say, sis.

CORY: And that's it.

I wouldn't be surprised if the next time he sees me is at *my* funeral.

I'm glad Mum wasn't there to see it. She would've been inconsolable.

The following week, my sister and I meet at Toowong Cemetery.

Two council workers to arrive and dig a shallow hole, only two feet down and one foot across—just wide enough for an ugly plastic box.

CORY *places the tub into the hole, picks up a fistful of hidden dirt from the hole ...*

And that's it.

We say nothing. No prayers. No rituals.

She scatters the dirt.

Just quietly arrange some lilies on top, then …

'Bye, Mum.'

'Bye.'

As if we're going down the road for a takeaway coffee.

We don't know what else to do …

Pause.

So we go down the road for a takeaway coffee.

I feel horrible we don't do better at farewelling Mum. I already know I'll always feel guilty about it.

Later, Shin clocks me ruminating over how little ceremony there was. How *lacking* it was.

He tells me that in Japan, mourners sort through the ashes of the dead, lifting bone fragments for closer examination; reading for signs.

I envy them. I envy Mediterranean widows who howl and weep. I envy Hindus, Jews and Muslims who wash the bodies of their dead.

The rest of us—agnostics, atheists—are left so … clueless.

Dying exposes the limitations of our lot like nothing else.

Beat.

The cancer has spread to my lymph nodes.

My sons are still in the dark.

I even hide my unhappiness from Shin.

I tell Shin that my writing is helping me—giving me something to focus on—when really I'm just at my desk, stuck and unable to write.

But he's been so supportive, it's the least I can do to pretend everything's fine.

So—god help me—I end up at the psychologist my doctor recommended.

THE PSYCHOLOGIST

PSYCH: **Welcome. Now. Have you heard of *mindfulness*?**

CORY: My psychologist speaks with a voice that suggests she's either reached enlightenment or has a prescription-painkiller dependency.

PSYCH: **It's *so* important to set aside time every day to just enjoy the small things, isn't it? The taste of an apple. The sound of babies laughing. The smell of rain …**

CORY: If I was paying for this, I might've asked for my money back.

But because it's free, I submit myself to this government-subsidised hostage situation to which I've voluntarily signed up.

PSYCH: **Now, Carrie.**

CORY: Cory.

PSYCH: **Kerry. Do you have any anxieties?**

CORY: Well. I'm anxious about dying.

PSYCH: **Oh, of course you are. That's normal. All feelings are valid.**

CORY: Well, you know. Dying. Seems like a big deal.

PSYCH: **Mm. Do you have any fears?**

CORY: Uh. Yes. Also dying.

The psychologist writes down 'dying' in her notes. She mouths the word 'dying' as she writes.

CORY *stares, then turns to the audience, unimpressed.*

I'm about to burst out of my skin, but it's not entirely her fault.

People like me expect more from psychologists than they can possibly deliver.

Especially when they say shit like:

PSYCH: **There's a great app I'd love to introduce you to!**

We hear the options:

This is whale song … waves …

And …

It sounds like a piss.

CORY: Urine?

PSYCH: **Babbling brook.**

More sounds. Shoes on gravel. Frogs. Guttural Tibetan throat singing.

CORY: It's getting weird.

When she asks about my feelings, I get the sense even *she* knows that she's last person I want to open up to.

PSYCH: **I'm sensing that I'm the last person you want to open up to.**

You don't have to share with me.

Let's try something else.

I want to you to close your eyes.

Getting up, now addressing audience:

Go on. Close your eyes.

If there's any hesitation:

(*I'm a clinical professional with multiple qualifications, please close your eyes.*)

The psychologist scans the room to ensure the audience has closed their eyes. She may stare audience members down if they don't comply.

Now imagine you're in a room full of strangers.

None of whom you know.

None of whom will see you again.

None of them will judge you.

Imagine you are there.

Now: in your mind, tell those strangers what you can't say out loud. What are you truly feeling?

We hear CORY*'s inner voice:*

CORY: Christ.

What *am* I feeling?

Well … I guess I'm sad.

(*Obviously.*)

Sad beyond belief, actually.

Maybe ashamed?

(*Why ashamed?*)

If I'm honest …

I've gone through life thinking death was something that happened to other people.

(*So deluded!*)

What else?

God, this is humiliating …

Am I … angry?

(*Of course I'm fucking angry.*)

'Why me?'

'Why now?'

'I was supposed to have an extra decade to do my best work! I was robbed! I'm a good writer! A good person! Jesus *Christ*, when I think of the number of arseholes and mediocre artists out there who are going to outlive me—!'

PSYCH: **Annnnd … open your eyes.**

It's okay to feel whatever you're feeling.

You've only just lost your mother.

These losses mount up.

What you're facing isn't little. It's monumental.

Death. It's the big one, Kirby.

EXIT INTERNATIONAL

Rolling her eyes at being misnamed, CORY *produces stick-on name tags and a permanent marker, and aggressively writes 'CORY' on one.*

CORY: I never see the psych again.

But she's made me realise: I *do* need to talk.

And she *was* right: I've only just lost my mother. I wouldn't want my sons carrying this guilt I feel; wouldn't want to leave behind a mess that shouldn't be theirs to clean up …

I get in touch with the local chapter of Exit International, the organisation that advocates for euthanasia.

It's funny. I've never been huge on clubs or memberships.

Especially ones that involve sharing your feelings.

Hanging with strangers, making small talk.

Can't think of anything worse.

But it's 2014, assisted dying isn't legal, and assisted suicide is construed as a criminal offence—and probably will be for as long as I'm alive.

So when I go to my first Exit International meeting, I'm a little nervous.

I meet 'Andrew' at the meeting. He's a handsome, healthy man.

She might slap a name tag on her: ANDREW.

ANDREW: **It's true.**

But inside, I'm a goddamn mess.

Rotten kidneys.

Horrible back.

Riddled with disease!

In an ideal world, I'd like to die by lethal injection.

You might think: 'sterile', 'clinical', 'what we do to animals' …

But if you saw how my old man died, you'd want to avoid the same fate too.

[*Suddenly cheery*] Anyway, you ready to learn the top-ten painless way to top yourselves?

CORY: It's a bit like a first-aid course in reverse, isn't it? It's confronting. Blunt. Slightly terrifying. But there's something thrilling and illicit too.

I also meet Carol.

Another name tag.

Physically, there's nothing technically the matter with Carol. In fact, she's the picture of rude health.

CAROL: **Twelve thousand steps today!**

CORY: But what you don't see is Carol has had an extremely tough life.

She's remarkably frank.

CAROL: **Years of abuse. Horrible husband.**

People ask, 'How do you find the strength to go on?' And I say:

'A cocktail of powerful anti-anxiety medication!'

'You're so strong!' they say.

[*Suddenly not strong*] But what if I don't want to be strong? Why can't I die painlessly, on my own terms, my dog by my side? Is that really so bad?

CORY: Maybe it's a reflex, but I almost feel it's our duty to tell Carol to keep going. Keep living!

But the more she talks, the more I can understand why she'd think, 'Why go on?'

And ironically … because we're all there for her …

She keeps showing up.

Then I meet Tom.

Another name tag.

Tom is nudging ninety. Oldest of the lot. But he's the prankster of the group, a loveable pest.

Right now, Tom is researching how he might take a helium bottle to the local cemetery to gas himself to death!

TOM: **Yeah look, no-one can be shocked or disgusted if they find my body there.**

After all …

CORY *inhales helium from a balloon:*

… it's the cemetery!

Everyone's already deeeeeeead!

CORY *prepares a cup of tea, fetches some biscuits.*

CORY: Oh, my turn? Hello, I'm Cory.

I'm a newcomer to death.

Ha. Suppose we all are.

When it comes to the method … I'm still unsure.

But … I imagine that once the day comes …

… maybe I'd invite my family …

… closest friends too …

… a farewell drink would be nice.

… Maybe some speeches, thanking everyone for everything they've done for me …

I'd tell them …

… I don't know, how much I love them. Too sappy?

… I reckon there'd be tears. Hopefully laughter too …

… and music from the soundtrack of my youth.

We hear—faintly—music from Cory's youth—e.g. 'Walk on By' by Dionne Warwick; 'Carolina in My Mind' by James Taylor; or 'Both Sides Now' by Joni Mitchell.

And then, when the time was right, maybe I'd say goodbye? Perhaps the party could go on without me …

Ha.

Can't think of a better way to go out.

SNAP. The lights change and CORY*'s back in the medical setting where numbers are being called out: '79' ... '80' ... '81' ...*

These meetings are so different from the hospital waiting room, where you sit alone, guarding your dirty little secret until your number's called.

I come out feeling diminished, like I've been reduced to my disease.

But here …

SNAP. The lights change back.

Here! We're like the last survivors on a sinking ship, huddled together for warmth and camaraderie through the worst, final storm.

And no, we're not all hell-bent on topping ourselves straight away.

Most of us probably won't.

But we have so little control anymore. This is our last act of reclaiming autonomy in the worst circumstances.

These meetings, these conversations … they might be about death …

But they're life-affirming.

EUTHANASIA DRUG

CORY: And they inspire me to get prepared, in case—or when—my illness suddenly accelerates.

I need to buy some drugs!

Anyone here a dealer? Sorry, does anyone 'know a drug dealer'?

Carol said I could travel to Mexico or Peru.

Apparently you just say you need to put down a sick horse.

I could get the drugs, drink them in my hotel room; let your family deal with shipping your remains home.

Orrrrrr … Andrew said you can get it online.

Drugs arrive to stage either via a drop or via the ASM dressed up as AusPost.

It's funny: I'd never broken the law in my life before this!

Now that I'm dying, I wonder if I should've broken it more.

(*Anyone here a cop? This never happened.*)

These drugs work fast. *Very* fast.

They'll go straight to the sleep centre of my brain in the time it takes me to say this sentence.

What would be easier than to swallow a fatal dose and never wake up again?

Preferable to all the alternatives.

SUICIDE NOTE

CORY: I write a suicide note, to my husband and sons.

'If I ever wake up from a surgery badly impaired, unable to walk, entirely dependent on other people to care for me, I'd prefer to end my own life …

And I want you to know …'

I hate the enormity of this task. But I'd also hate for my final words with them to be something flippant and banal.

How do you distil how much someone means to you? Or why you've had to do this?

She continues writing.

'Sorry. Please forgive me.

Talk to me when I'm gone. I'll be listening.'

Is that even how it works?

It all feels so inadequate.

Frustration. She crosses out the lines. Stuck, she appeals …

There's still so much I want to say to Shin. To my sons. So many stories they don't even know.

Parts of my life I haven't thought about in years. They know nothing about so many …

Chapters.

And I *am* a writer.

Writing, even if you're only doing it in your head, shapes the world and makes it bearable.

There's still time to tell these stories.

There's still time to finish one final book.

Not a novel.

A memoir. I know the subject. Maybe even the title.

There's still time.

And in a sudden rush, I find myself writing …

About our airline pilot father, who we always called Captain Taylor—who had such a problem with authority, he was thrown out of the airforce … which probably saved his life given all the other trainees blown to bits over Germany …

About our childhood trips to the family sheep and cattle property near Barcaldine; visits to all those pesky relatives who thought my university-educated mother was too full of dangerous ideas …

The sound of howling wind.

About our childhood in Fiji, where we lived with my mother when a hurricane approached …

Rain. Thunder. Shutters shaking in the storm.

How my mother and I rushed around in swimsuits to ready the house …

How the hurricane approached; the rain coming down in walls of water …

How my mother found hurricane shutters stored under the house and fetched a ladder …

FIJI & NEAR DEATH

The sounds of rain, thunder and howling winds crescendo.

CORY: The storm was wild.

My job: to hand the hurricane shutters to my mother one by one. Heavier than you'd expect.

She scooped me into a blanket, trying to shield us from the noise.

The wind whipped and lashed the garden in all directions at once …

We were so small and pathetic in the face of nature's rage.

Lights and sound increasingly falter, like the show is experiencing a technical glitch.

All day and all night it continued.

It was too loud to hear each other. So I took hold of Mum's hand and communicated my love for her that way. And anyway, words seemed inadequate.

In the rage of the storm:

I remember thinking that Mum looked as terrified as us. That's when it struck me: 'Mothers can't protect you from everything.'

So there was nothing else to do but cling to each other for courage and warmth.

The hurricane descended. There was no stopping it.

All we had was each other.

As the lights strobe and the audio falters, CORY *winces and holds onto her forehead in pain, like she's experiencing the onset of a migraine. She reaches out as if to her mother.*

In amongst the hurricane, we also begin to hear:

Heart monitors ...

Assisted breathing ...

Hospital sounds ...

The strobe lightning becomes more chaotic and difficult to watch.

And then, suddenly: calm.

The lighting is strange, somewhere between awake and sleep.

CORY *looks back at the audience as the light fades into complete darkness.*

It's late December 2014.

Years since I was properly diagnosed.

A seizure leaves me helpless as a baby.

A tumour in my brain requires surgery.

It's a terrible thing to admit, but before going under, I'm so scared by how this could leave me, that I half-hope I don't wake up.

A FAMILY MEETING

CORY*'s face returns to us in the darkness—but just her face.*

CORY: But I do.
Good news: the brain tumour's gone.
Bad news: they've run out of treatment options.
I don't come out of the operation unimpaired, either.

Lights expand, revealing CORY *now using a cane. She may wear a hospital gown. Her body is changed and so is her gait.*

I have a shower.
Catch a glimpse of myself in the mirror.
Like a flash; an apparition.
Have you ever looked in the mirror and seen an intruder—
Only to realise it's you?
It's *my* body in the mirror.
Overnight, my body has become alien.
It's so frightening, so incomprehensible, that this is *me* now.
There's no coming back from this.
I thought I was brave.
But now I'm face-to-face with this.
Her.
Me.
There's nowhere to hide.
No way to deny the obvious.
No way to shield anyone from what's happening to me.
So I convene a family meeting in our home.
There's me, my husband, our sons, their partners.
Nat lives overseas. I summon him back; he knows it's serious.
And because I've withheld so much, I now have to spill everything, answering all their questions at once:
[*In rapid succession, to an audience member*] It's cancer, yes.
[*To another audience member*] Melanoma. Stage four.
[*To another audience member*] No, it's not good.
[*To another audience member*] Yes, terminal.

[*To another audience member*] No, Nat.

[*To another audience member*] Yes, Dan.

[*To another audience member*] Yes, your dad's known all along.

[*To another audience member*] Shin, teishi [stop]—they're allowed to feel what they're feeling.

[*To another audience member*] I know. I should've. But I didn't. And I'm sorry.

[*To another audience member*] Yes, Nat. We've gotten second opinions.

[*To another audience member*] And third. And fourth.

[*To another audience member*] No, Dan. I wish.

[*To another audience member*] Well, you know: melanoma's notoriously unpredictable. But it's everywhere now.

[*To another audience member*] Christmas would be good. Yeah.

[*To entire audience*] They're taken aback. I feel so terrible for doing this to them.

I know it's ridiculous, but that's how it feels: like I've *done* this *to* them.

They disguise what they're feeling well, but I'd forgive their anger, rage, despair … I just wish I could take it away from them.

We go through all the paperwork they need to access if—when—the worst happens.

Tonnes of paperwork fall from the ceiling in distinct colours. Some might fall on the audience. As she starts to collect it all and organise it into colour-coded piles ...

(*So much goddamn paperwork when you're dying.*)

She struggles with it. An audience member may help.

(*Thank you.*)

The documents that build throughout a life …

Tax. Superannuation. Bank statements.

Home insurance. Health insurance. Life insurance.

Power of attorney. Will. Passwords.

(*So many passwords. If the cancer doesn't kill me, two-factor authentication will.*)

But it helps me to feel like I am putting my house in order.

And I think it helps them, because it makes them feel useful.

We discuss the euthanasia drugs. I refer to it as my Marilyn Monroe gift pack.

'If it was good enough for her, it's good enough for me.'

(*They don't get the joke.*)

I explain that even if I never use it, knowing it's there gives me a sense of control.

To the extent that they don't object, I can only hope they understand.

AN APPARITION

CORY: I live with pain as a constant companion now.

Night and day, my stash calls to me, like an secret lover.

Let me take you away from all this, it whispers.

But even if I had it, I'd have to take it alone—miserably alone.

Any sniff of Shin or my sons helping me, and they'd be facing jail.

I can't understand how, for as long as I'll be alive, the law stops me from choosing an assisted death.

I hate that my death certificate would read 'suicide' as 'cause of death'. The fact that cancer actually killed me would be completely lost. No-one would know.

So many conversations about practicalities, reform, legalities, law.

Has anyone ever thought to ask the dying what they think and need?

Then: somehow the country's biggest writers' festival gets wind of the fact I'm writing this memoir. And I'm invited to speak.

(*Ha!*)

I'm too weak to fly to Sydney.

We arrange for me to dial-in, instead.

When it's announced, hundreds upon hundreds of people register for the event. It sells out quickly; they move it to a bigger venue.

Turns out, people *do* want to have this conversation.

And with a dying woman, no less.

SYDNEY WRITERS' FESTIVAL

CORY: The session is titled, 'What makes a good death?' My fellow panelists are a doctor who has treated people at the end of their lives.

PHYSICIAN: [*smarmy*] Pleasure to be here.

CORY: And a well-known broadcaster and assisted dying advocate.

ADVOCATE: [*Andrew Denton-ly*] Thanks for having me.

CORY: And there's me: the dying woman. Well, that's not how I'm introduced. But the audience is told I'm joining via audio link, as my health prevents me from being there. And that I'm currently writing a book named *Dying: A Memoir*.

Beat.

I think they can connect the dots.

The doctor starts:

DOCTOR: Well, it's good that the Australian Medical Association is finally saying, 'We need to talk more about the last taboo.' The conversation is starting.

ADVOCATE: Only just starting, doctor? People have been dying for *quite* some time. I'm not saying it's your fault; the problem is structural. But people are dying, right now.

CORY: Yes! And can I add—

DOCTOR: Look, I am sympathetic. But the idea of a euthanasia wing in a hospital? I can't get my head around that! If doctor-assisted suicide is law, we'll have an obligation to kill.

CORY: Not quite though, it's more—

ADVOCATE: What do you mean by 'obligation to kill'? You are supplying somebody with the choice to end their suffering. How is that—by any definition—killing?

CORY: Agreed! See, in my experience—

DOCTOR: But in my training and mindset, which saves lives, it feels like killing!

CORY: Oh, honestly—

ADVOCATE: Then your mindset needs to change!

CORY: Is anyone going to let me—

DOCTOR: **It's important we're starting this conversation, but …**

CORY: That's when I lose it.

[*Shouting down the phone line*] How long is 'this conversation' supposed to take?! Some of us don't have that luxury of time.

I understand the dilemma. But as somebody who's dying—right now, ME—the idea that I'm asking you to kill me …

Just to put it in those terms seems ludicrous to me! I'm sorry, but …

You're actually helping me to die—which is something *that is happening to me anyway*.

And I hesitate to say I'd die from a 'natural death' because it won't be natural. It'll be assisted—by *all kinds of medications*.

The effects of which I have NO idea about.

I'll be at the mercy of whoever's giving me these doses of … whatever they're giving me.

I don't understand what they're doing.

Some of those will clearly hasten my death anyway.

But to describe assisted dying as 'killing' or 'murder'!

No sense!

It just makes no sense to me.

NONE.

A tense beat. Maybe a cough.

DOCTOR: **[*sheepishly*] Uh … shall we take some audience questions?**

DYING

CORY: My doctor had said things would move slowly, and then, very fast.

But it still catches me off guard exactly *how* fast. Ten years, gone—just like that.

No getting out of this now.

At the same time, I hadn't anticipated how slow the days would be.

This is my world now.

The bathroom.

The living room.

The bedroom.

I'm like an infant.

I lie around.

Dream.

Day bleeds into night.

I sleep during the day, when everyone's awake.

I'm awake at night, when everyone's asleep.

The rhythms of the day don't exist like they once did.

I write. Or try to. I move between rooms.

I sleep.

I sleep so much, more and more, with every passing day.

Is this what death is, in the end?

Me, just sleeping more and more, until it's permanent?

A slow retreat from consciousness, back to the oblivion that came before it?

The psychologist was right about one thing: the losses do mount up.

Sometimes, from the confinement of my bed and the sofa—when I'm being 'mindful', I guess—I'll be distracted by the sight of people passing by outside.

I envy them. All of them.

Couples out for an evening walk. Passing cyclists, gliding along—the way I used to.

People driving—something I've had to give up after surgery.

(*I even miss road-rage. God, I'd love to verbally abuse a stranger I'll never see again.*)

CORY *directs some road-rage at a member of the audience.*

(*We haven't met, have we?*)

(*GOOD. PICK A LANE!*)

There's an endless list of pleasures I can no longer enjoy!

How could I have known it would be my final time: driving, cycling, walking? Should I have celebrated and marked the moment?

Or was it better not to know?

My palliative care specialist initially refers me to a Catholic facility.

The crucifix appears.

Absolutely not.

The crucifix disappears.

So we opt for one run by Buddhists instead.

My passport expires. I'll never go back to Japan.

FINAL ANSWERS

CORY: And … that's it. Everything sorted.

(*Apparently.*)

Paperwork. Death admin. No medical questions left to ask.

Aren't I supposed to be at peace now?

To be honest, I'm more terrified than ever.

And I have all these questions, none of which have definitive answers.

She steps into the audience.

[*To audience member*] Do you mind if I ask you some?

[*To audience member*] ***Are you scared of death?***

IF YES:

(*Yes! Thank you! So am I! God, this is good to say out loud!*)

IF NO:

(*You're on something, aren't you? It's okay, I won't tell. But can I have some?*)

[*To audience member*] (*Oh, I like this.*)

[*To audience member*] ***Are you a dog or cat person?***

IF DOG:

(*But there's so much poo. And you have to pick it up while it's still warm ...*)

IF CAT:

(*They're cute aren't they, but you know they'd murder you in your sleep if they could ...*)

[*To audience member*] ***Do you think duck is—quote—a 'dirty, disgusting bird'?***

IF YES:

(*You'd really get along with my brother.*)

IF NO:

(*Right? My brother obviously needs help.*)

[*To audience member*] ***If an animal were in pain, could you euthanise it?***

IF YES:

(*So you're a cold-blooded murderer. Take this* [*the drugs*], *I might need your assistance later ...*)

IF NO:

(*So you'd prefer an animal to die slowly and painfully. Good to know ... Chilling.*)

[*To audience member*] ***Do you say eutha-nayz or euthan-eyez?***

EITHER WAY:

(*Honestly, who cares about proper pronunciation at this stage? Life's too short. I should know.*)

[*To audience member*] ***Have you heard of mindfulness?***

IF YES:

(*You're in cahoots with that psychologist, aren't you?*)

IF NO:

(*It's fine to remain in the dark. But if you're interested, there's an app.*)

[*To audience member*] ***Have you ever used the phrase 'live-laugh-love' unironically?***

IF YES:

(*Absolutely not going to your palliative care centre, no offence.*)

IF NO:

(*But you've whispered it to yourself in a private moment, haven't you?*)

[*To audience member*] ***Are you a cop?***

IF YES:

([*hides drugs*] *You didn't see anything.*)

IF NO:

(*Good* [*re: drugs*]*—we can split this.*)

[*To audience member*] ***Where could you happily die?***

IF A LOVELY ANSWER:

(*Wow, you have really thought about this. Take me with you!*)

IF A WEIRD ANSWER:

(*I was not expecting that. And I regret asking the question.*)

[*To audience member*] ***Burial or cremation?***

IF BURIAL:

(*I respect that. Take it from me: you can't trust your family with your ashes.*)

IF CREMATION:

(*I respect that. But take it from me: you can't always trust your family with your ashes.*)

IF A THIRD OPTION:

(*I said ... Burial or cremation.*)

[*To audience member*] ***Do you believe in the afterlife?***

IF NO:

(*Yeah, neither do I.*)

IF YES:

(*Do you? Wow, I love that. I'm a little jealous, actually. Because:*)

I honestly just believe we come from nothingness; we return to nothingness. It feels obvious to me. Sad as all hell. But obvious.

It's funny: on our last visit to Arita, Shin told me that he liked to think that in centuries from now, his own porcelain would be found, like the shards we found in the cemeteries. It's his idea of immortality.

I think … I feel the same about my writing.

And that maybe long after I'm gone… someone might read something of mine and be touched in some way.

One of my novels. An essay I've written. This memoir.

Huh. Maybe I *do* believe in the afterlife.

A MEMOIR

CORY: It *was* a lonely business, dying.

But turns out … it doesn't need to be that way.

We often ask ourselves: what constitutes a life well-lived?

But what constitutes a good death?

We convince ourselves it's impossible to confront it:

— 'I can't see that psych.'

— 'I can't face the paperwork.'

— 'I can't do palliative care.'

But trust me. You'll show up for it. Be present for it. Sit with it.

I know you will.

Because you've *already* done that with me. And *you*, and *you*, and *you*.

What did I tell you? That I'd invite you all over when the day came.

The lights come up on the audience a little more overtly. Perhaps the song from her youth starts to play.

Harold Pinter once wrote, 'I shall miss you so much when I'm dead.'

I know what he means.

I'll miss my husband of thirty-one years.

I'll miss the faces of my sons.

I'll miss my sister. My brother.

(*To an extent.*)

I'll miss the world and everything in it.

I'll miss … *this.*

The world meets the audience. A pause, in amongst the wonder:

I'm only grateful I tasted so much of it when I had the chance.

But I won't miss dying. There is nothing good about dying. It is sad beyond belief. But it is part of life, and there is no escaping it. Once you grasp that fact, good things can result. But it's by far the hardest thing I've ever done. And I'll be glad when it's over.

I'd like to be remembered though. For what I've written.

Which, by the way, I did finish my final book. My publishers fast-track its publication, so I can see it while I'm still alive.

I launch it via Skype. The first edition gets an endorsement from Julian Barnes.

Booker Prize-winner Julian fucking Barnes!

He never endorses anyone.

When he sends over the endorsement, I write to my editor:

'Tell Julian it's worth getting cancer to get such accolades.'

Julian writes back to my editor:

'Tell her no, actually. But thanks for the thought.'

My publishers hope the book will come out in America.

Who knows if anyone will read it there.

Whatever happens, I won't be here to see it.

I have no real say in any of this. None of us do.

All I know is it's time for me to say goodbye, knowing that the party will go on without me.

Can't think of a better way to go out.

Lights out.

EPILOGUE

The ACTOR *returns.*

ACTOR: Cory Taylor died on the fifth of July, 2016, at Karuna, a Buddhist hospice in Queensland, her family by her side. Although she didn't expect to make it past her sixtieth birthday, she died aged sixty-one.

Dying: A Memoir is the fastest book Cory's publishers ever released. She didn't get to see its American release, which was endorsed by Hilary Mantel, praised in the *New York Times*, and selected by Barack Obama as one of his Top Ten Books of the Year.

Nearly a decade on, voluntary assisted dying is legal in all Australian states. But there are still barriers to access. It remains illegal in the Northern Territory, and doctors are prohibited from even raising it as an option in South Australia.

Silence and stigma make discussing death—and what we want for ourselves when we die—even harder. But Cory showed us the value of talking about death, while we're still here.

The ACTOR *picks up a copy of the book* Dying: A Memoir*, by Cory Taylor.*

This is Cory Taylor, writing about the publication of her debut novel, in *Dying: A Memoir.*

The ACTOR *reads from the book:*

'A sudden death cuts out all of the ghastly preliminaries, but I imagine it leaves behind a terrible regret for all the things left permanently unspoken. A slow death, like mine, has that one advantage …

You have a lot of time to talk, to tell people how you feel, to try to make sense of the whole thing …

… of the life that is coming to a close, both for yourself and for those who remain.'

THE END

ALTERNATIVE EXTRACTS:

'This is what I'm doing now, in this, my final book: I am making a shape for my death, so that I, and others, can see it clearly. And I am making dying bearable for myself. I don't know where I would be if I couldn't do this strange work. It has saved my life so many times over the years, and it continues to do so now. For while my body is careering towards catastrophe, my mind is elsewhere, concentrated on this other, vital task, which is to tell you something meaningful before I go.'

'So much sweetness is bound to leave a terrible void when it's gone. I'm only grateful I tasted so much of it when I had the chance. I have had a blessed life in that way, full of countless delights. When you're dying, even your unhappiest memories can induce a sort of fondness, as if delight is not confined to the good times, but is woven through your days, like a skein of gold thread.'

NEXTSTAGE

Commissioned and developed through Melbourne Theatre Company's NEXT STAGE Writers' Program with the support of our Current and Inaugural Playwrights Giving Circles.

NEXT STAGE positions new Australian works as contenders on the national stage, through strategic investment in stories that reflect our community, are relevant to our times, challenge the boundaries of theatre making and fuel the cultural conversation.

Thank you for sharing our passion and commitment to Australian stories and Australian writers.

PLAYWRIGHTS GIVING CIRCLE

Thank you to Melbourne Theatre Company's Playwrights Giving Circle – its donors, foundations and organisations – for sharing our passion and commitment to Australian stories and writers.

Tony and Janine Burgess, Fitzpatrick Sykes Family Foundation, Jane Hansen AO & Paul Little AO, Larry Kamener & Petra Kamener, Susanna Mason, Helen Nicolay, Pimlico Foundation, Tania Seary & Chris Lynch, Craig Semple, Dr Richard Simmie, Andrew Sisson AO & Tracey Sisson, Caroline Young & Derek Young AM

INAUGURAL PLAYWRIGHTS GIVING CIRCLE

Louise Myer & Martyn Myer AO, Maureen Wheeler AO & Tony Wheeler AO, Christine Brown Bequest, Allan Myers AC KC & Maria Myers AC, Tony Burgess & Janine Burgess, Dr Andrew McAliece & Dr Richard Simmie, Larry Kamener & Petra Kamener

NAOMI
MILGROM
FOUNDATION

Melbourne Theatre Company

BOARD OF MANAGEMENT
Chair Martin Hosking
Deputy Chair Leigh O'Neill
Tony Johnson
Larry Kamener
Katerina Kapobassis
Sally Noonan
Chris Oliver-Taylor
Tiriki Onus
Anne-Louise Sarks
Craig Semple
Professor Marie Sierra
Tania Seary

FOUNDATION BOARD
Chair Tania Seary
Deputy Chair Jane Grover
Karen Cusack
Charles Gillies
Jane Grover
Sally Lansbury
Sally Noonan
Rupert Sherwood
Tracey Sisson

EXECUTIVE MANAGEMENT
Artistic Director & Co-CEO
Anne-Louise Sarks
Executive Director & Co-CEO
Sally Noonan
Executive Producer & Deputy CEO
Martina Murray
Artistic Administrator
Olivia Brewer
Executive Administrator
Kathleen Ashby

ARTISTIC
Associate Artists
Tasnim Hossain
Jean Tong
Mark Wilson
Head of New Work
Jennifer Medway
New Work Associate
Zoey Dawson
Resident Dramaturg
Isobel Morphy-Walsh
Playwriting Fellow
Alistair Baldwin

CASTING
Casting Director
Janine Snape
Casting Administrator
Daphne Quah

PRODUCING
Senior Producer
Stephen Moore
Producer – Industry & Audience Initiatives
Laura Harris
Company Manager
Julia Smith
Deputy Company Manager
Blaze Bryans

DEVELOPMENT
Director of Development
Rupert Sherwood
Senior Philanthropy Manager
Sophie Boardley
Annual Giving Manager
Meaghan Donaldson
Philanthropy Coordinator
Charlotte Menzies-King
Business Development Manager
José Ortiz
Partnerships Manager
Isobel Lake

EDUCATION & FAMILIES
Director of Education & Families (Acting)
Nick Tranter
Education Content Producer
Emily Doyle
Deadly Creatives Project Officer
Emma Holgate
Schools Engagement Project Officer
Izabella Yena
Education Access Project Officer
Teresa Moore

PEOPLE & CULTURE
Director of People & Culture
Joanna Geysen
People & Culture Business Partner
Maddison Ryan
Receptionist
David Zierk

FINANCE & IT
Director of Finance & IT
Rob Pratt
Finance Manager
Andrew Slee
Assistant Accountant
Nicole Chong
IT & Systems Manager
Michael Schuettke
IT Support Officer
Darren Snowdon
Payroll Officer
Julia Godinho
Payments Officer
Harper St Clair
Building Services Manager
Adrian Aderhold

MARKETING & COMMUNICATIONS
Director of Marketing & Communications
Chris MacDonald
Head of Marketing
Claire La Greca
Marketing Campaign Manager
Aayushi Parikh
Program Marketing & Activation Lead
Rebecca Lawrence
Marketing & Communications Coordinator
Matisse Knight
Digital Engagement Manager
Jane Sutherland
Digital Coordinator
Harrison Buikstra
Lead Graphic Designer /Art Director
Kate Francis
Graphic Designer
Sarah Ridgway-Cross
Head of Communications
Isabella Ramdhanie
Communications Manager
Tilly Graovac
Video Content Producer
Harvey Newland-Harman
Publicity Consultant
Good Humans PR

PRODUCTION
Director of Technical & Production
Adam J Howe
Senior Production Manager
Michele Preshaw
Production Managers
Suzy Brooks
Jess Maguire
Margaret Murray
Production Administrator
Alyson Brown
Production Coordinator
Zoe Rabb
Production Assistant
Elysia Harris
Technical Manager – Electrics
Allan Hirons
Technical Coordinators – Electrics
Nic Wollan
Max Wilkie
Production Technician Operator
Marcus Cook
Production Technicians
Max Bowyer
Stella Dandolo
Claire Ferguson
Scott McAllister
Sidney Millar
Natalya Shield
Ounie Witherow Aitken
Technical Manager – Staging & Design
Andrew Bellchambers
Production Design Coordinator
Jacob Battista
Head Mechanist
Tobias Chesworth

PROPERTIES
Properties Supervisor
Geoff McGregor
Props Maker
Colin Penn
Props Buyer
Finn McLeish

SCENIC ART
Scenic Art Supervisor
Shane Dunn
Scenic Artist
Alison Crawford
Colin Harman
Nellie Summerfield

WORKSHOP
Workshop Supervisor
Andrew Weavers
Set Makers
Sarah Hall
Nick Gray
Philip De Mulder
Peter Rosa
Simon Juliff
Welder
Ken Best

COSTUME
Costume Manager
Kate Seeley
Costume Staff
Jocelyn Creed
Lyn Molloy
John Van Gastel
Costume Coordinator
Carletta Childs
Millinery
Phillip Rhodes
Costume Hire
Liz Symonds
Costume Maintenance
Jodi Hope
Claire Munnings
Art Finishing
Alicia Aulsebrook
Claire Mercer

STAGE MANAGEMENT
Head of Stage Management
Whitney McNamara
Stage Managers
Annie Gleisner
Mercedes Gowlett
Rain Iyahen
Annah Jacobs
Juliette Hirons
Jess Keepence
Jenny Le
Finn McLeish
Zsuzsa Gaynor Mihaly
Tom O' Sullivan
Lisa Osborn
Brittany Stock
Pippa Wright

SOUTHBANK THEATRE
Events Manager
Mandy Jones
Production Services Manager
Frank Stoffels
Front of House Manager
Drew Thomson
Lighting Supervisor
Geoff Adams-Walsh
Deputy Lighting Supervisor
Tom Roach
Sound Supervisor
Joy Weng
Deputy Sound Supervisor
Will Patterson
Fly/Staging Supervisor
Adam Hanley
Deputy Fly Supervisor
Callum O'Connor
Stage & Technical Staff
Jon Bargen
Ash Basham
Al Brill
Suzy Brooks
Sam Bruechert
Emily Campbell
Steve Campbell
Will Campbell
Bryan Chin
Kit Cunneen
Jeremy Fowlie
Justin Heaton
Spencer Herd
Chris Hubbard
Ethan Hunter
Marcus Macris
Alexandre Malta
Jason Markoutsas
Terry McKibbin
David Membery
Sharna Murphy
Alix Otenstein
Jake Rogers
Natalya Shield
Nathaniel Sy
Tom Vulcan
Dylan Wainwright-Berrell
House Supervisors
George Abbott
Tanya Batt
Matt Bertram
Kasey Gambling
House Attendants
Rhiannon Atkinson-Howatt
Stephanie Barham
Emily Bosch
Briannah Borg
Zak Brown
Sam Diamond
Liz Drummond
Grace Ephraums
Leila Gerges
Hugo Gutteridge
Abby Hampton
Kate Hannah
Michael Hart
Elise Jansen
Kathryn Joy
Sophia Maltarollo
Natasha Milton
Ernesto Munoz
Brooke Painter
Lucy Pembroke
Brigid Quonoey
Taylor Reece
Solomon Rumble
Sophie Scott
Mieke Singh Dodd
Ayesha Tauseef
Olivia Walker
Rhian Wilson

TICKETING
Director of Ticketing Operations
Brenna Sotiropoulos
Customer Service Sales Manager
Jessie Phillips
VIP Ticketing Officer
Michael Bingham
Education Ticketing Officer
Mellita Ilich
Subscriptions & Telemarketing Team Leader
Peter Dowd
Ticketing Services Administrator
Hannah Flannery
Box Office Supervisors
Darcy Fleming (leave cover)
Bridget Mackey
Tain Stangret
Box Office Attendants
Stephanie Barham
Tanya Batt
Britt Ferry
Casey Gould
Min Kingham
Julia Landberg
Julie Leung
Brigid Meredith
Michael Stratford Hutch
Lee Threadgold
Rhian Wilson

CRM & AUDIENCE INSIGHTS
Director of CRM & Audience Insights
Jeremy Hodgins
Database Specialist
Ben Gu
Data Analyst
Sionna Maple

COMMISSIONS
The Joan & Peter Clemenger Commissions
Kylie Coolwell
NEXT STAGE Commissions
Van Badham
Kamarra Bell-Wykes
Andrew Bovell
Angus Cerini
Patricia Cornelius
Declan Furber Gillick
Sheridan Harbridge
Claudia Karvan
Michele Lee
Glenn Moorhouse
Kate Mulvaney
Joe Paradise Lui
Leah Purcell
Sally Sara
S. Shakthidharan
Melanie Tait
Aran Thangaratnam

Our Donors

We gratefully acknowledge the ongoing support of our leading Donors.

LIFETIME PATRONS

Acknowledging a lifetime of extraordinary support.

Rowland Ball OAM & The Late Monica Maughan
Pat Burke
Peter Clemenger AO & The Late Joan Clemenger AO
Greig Gailey & Dr Geraldine Lazarus
Allan Myers AC KC & Maria Myers AC
The Late Biddy Ponsford
The Late Dr Roger Riordan AM
Maureen Wheeler AO & Tony Wheeler AO
The Late Ursula Whiteside
Caroline Young & Derek Young AM

ENDOWMENT FUND DONORS

Supporting Melbourne Theatre Company's long-term sustainability and creative future.

Leading Gifts

Jane Hansen AO & Paul Little AO

$50,000+

John Higgins AO & Jodie Maunder
Martin & Loreto Hosking

$20,000+

Prudence & Neil Morrison
Andrew Sisson AO & Tracey Sisson

$10,000+

Helen Lynch AM & Helen Bauer
Jennifer Darbyshire & David Walker
Charles Gilles & Penny Allen
Ian Hicks AO
Tony & Nathalie Johnson
Tania Seary & Chris Lynch
Craig Semple

PLAYWRIGHTS GIVING CIRCLE

Supporting the NEXT STAGE Writers' Program, our industry-leading commissioning initiative.

Tony & Janine Burgess, Fitzpatrick Sykes Family Foundation, Jane Hansen AO & Paul Little AO, Larry Kamener & Petra Kamener, Susanna Mason, Helen Nicolay, Pimlico Foundation, Tania Seary & Chris Lynch, Craig Semple, Dr Richard Simmie, Andrew Sisson AO & Tracey Sisson, Caroline Young & Derek Young AM

TRUSTS & FOUNDATIONS

The Gailey Lazarus Foundation

Annual giving

Acknowledging Donors whose recent gifts help enrich and transform lives through the magic of theatre.

Current as of July 2025.

BENEFACTORS CIRCLE

$50,000+

APS Foundation
Krystyna Campbell-Pretty AM
Peter Clemenger AO
The Cybec Foundation
Fitzpatrick Sykes Family Foundation
The Helen Fraser Giving Fund
Greig Gaily & Dr Geraldine Lazarus
Jane Hansen AO & Paul Little AO
Martin & Loreto Hosking
Tania Seary & Chris Lynch
Andrew Sisson AO & Tracey Sisson
Maureen Wheeler AO & Tony Wheeler AO

$20,000+

Tony & Janine Burgess
The Glenholme Foundation
Petra & Larry Kamener
Craig Semple
Orcadia Foundation LTD
The John & Myriam Wylie Foundation
The Vizard Foundation

$10,000+

Alan & Mary-Louise Archibald Foundation
John & Lorraine Bates
Jay Bethell & Peter Smart
Michael Buxton AM & Janet Buxton
Angie & Colin Carter
The Cattermole Family
Jennifer Darbyshire & David Walker
The Dowd Foundation
Linda Herd
Diane John
Daryl Kendrick & Leong Lai Peng (Betty)
Helen Lynch AM & Helen Bauer
Susanna Mason
Ian & Margaret McKellar
Helen Nicolay
Pimlico Foundation
Catherine Quealy
The Reid Malley Foundation
Lisa Ring
Anne & Mark Robertson OAM
The Robert Salzer Foundation
Dr Richard Simmie
Rob Stewart & Lisa Dowd
Tintagel Bay P/L
Ralph Ward-Ambler AM & Barbara Ward-Ambler
Anonymous (1)

$5,000+

Joanna Baevski
Bagôt Gjergja Foundation
James Best & Doris Young
Dr Douglas Brown & Treena Brown
Dr Andrew Buchanan & Peter Darcy
Bill Burdett AM & Sandra Burdett
Pat Burke & Jan Nolan
Diana Burleigh
Alison & John Cameron
Ann Cutts
Prof Glyn Davis AC & Prof Margaret Gardner AC
Marian Evans
Patricia Faulkner AO
Christine Gilbertson
Charles Gilles & Penny Allen
Roger & Jan Goldsmith
Lesley Griffin
David & Lilly Harris
David & Lilly Harris
Jane Hemstritch AO
Tony Hillery & Warwick Eddington
Amy & Paul Jasper
Jane Kunstler
Martin & Melissa McIntosh
George & Rosa Morstyn
The Myer Foundation
Tom & Ruth O'Dea
Leigh O'Neill
Dr Kia Pajouhesh (Smile Solutions)
Jeremy Ruskin & Roz Zalewski
Lynne Sherwood
Trawalla Foundation Trust
Janet Whiting AM & Phil Lukies
Anonymous (5)

ADVOCATES CIRCLE

$2,500+

Nan Brown
Ian & Jillian Buchanan
Lynne & Rob Burgess
Geoff Cosgriff
Ann Darby
Megan Davis
Rodney Dux
Anna & John Field
Nigel & Cathy Garrard
Diana & Murray Gerstman
Heather & Bob Glindemann OAM
Jane Grover
Peter & Halina Jacobsen
Alex Lewenberg
Libby McMeekin
Sandra Murdoch
Jane & Andrew Murray
Nelson Bros Funeral Services
Dr Paul Nisselle AM & Sue Nisselle
Dr John Sime
Geoff Steinicke
James & Anne Syme
David & Angela Taft
Liz Tromans
The Veith Foundation
Kaye & John de Wijn
Price & Christine Williams
The Ray & Margaret Wilson Foundation
Gillian & Tony Wood
Anonymous (3)

LOYALTY CIRCLE

$1,000+

Prof Noel Alpins AM & Sylvia Alpins
Margaret Astbury
Ian Baker & Cheryl Saunders
Prof Robin Batterham
Judy Bourke
Jenny & Lucinda Brash
Bernadette Broberg
Beth Brown & The Late Tom Bruce AM
Jannie Brown
Julie Burke
Katie Burke
John & Jan Campbell
Jessica Canning
Jenny & Stephen Charles AO
Susan Cohen
Sandy & Yvonne Constantine
Deborah Conyngham
Karen Cusack
Sue & John Denmead
Mark Duckworth PSM & Lauren Mosso
Dr Sally Duguid & Dr David Tingay
Pam Durrant
Bev & Geoff Edwards
Karen & David Elias
Nita Eng
Dr Alastair Fearn
Paul & Mary Fildes
Bruce Freeman
Gaye & John Gaylard
Fiona Griffiths & Tony Osmond
Gill Family Foundation
Ian & Wendy Haines
Luke Heagerty
Ian & Titania Henderson Foundation
Lorraine Hendrata
Brett & Kerri Hereward
Howard & Glennys Hocking
Amelia Holland
Emeritus Prof Andrea Hull AO
Nanette Hunter
Sally & Rod Johnstone
Lesley & Ian Jones
Leah Kaplan & Barry Levy
Irene Kearsey & Michael Ridley
Malcolm Kemp
Fiona Kirwan-Hamilton & Brett Parkin
Doris & Steve Klein
Marianne & Arthur Klepfisz
Larry Kornhauser OAM & Natalya Gill
S Lansbury & D Di Fabio
Verona Lea
Alison & Jim Leslie
Glenda & Greg Lewin AM
Peter & Judy Loney
Lord Family
Kerryn Lowe & Raphael Arndt
Ken & Jan Mackinnon
Karin MacNab
Natasha & Laurence Mandie
Chris Maple
Ian & Judi Marshman
Colin & Helen Masters
Penelope McEniry
Heather & Simon McKeon
Paula McKinnon & Troy Sussman
Garry McLean
Emeritus Prof Peter McPhee AM
Robert & Helena Mestrovic
Barbara & David Mushin
Sarah Nguyen
Nick Nichola & Ingrid Moyle
Michele Nielsen
Dr Rosemary Nixon AM
Dr Jane & Alan Oppenheim
In loving memory of Richard Park
Bruce Parncutt AO
Dr Annamarie Perlesz
Dare & Andrea Power
Philip & Gayle Raftery
David Reckenberg & Dale Bradbury
Sally Redlich
Victoria Redwood
Christopher Reed
John & Veronica Rickard
Ken & Gail Roche
Roslyn & Richard Rogers Family
S & S Rogerson
B & J Rollason
Nick & Rowena Rudge
Jeremy Ruskin & Roz Zalewski
Edwina Sahhar
Margaret Sahhar AM
Sandi Foundation dedicated to Alec
FE Scott
Sally & Tim Scott
Susan Selwyn & Barry Novy
Jacky & Rupert Sherwood
Diane Silk
Pauline & Tony Simioni
Jan Simon
Jane Simon & Peter Cox
Rachel Slade
Tim & Angela Smith
Annette Smorgon
Brian Snape AM & Christina Martin
Dr Ross & Helen Stillwell
Rosemary Stipanov
The Stirling Family
Shannon Super
Irene & John Sutton
Rodney & Aviva Taft
Frank Tisher OAM & Dr Miriam Tisher
John & Anna van Weel
Kevin & Elizabeth Walsh
Ann & Alan Wilkinson
Mandy & Edward Yencken
Anonymous (22)

SUPPORTER CIRCLE

$100+

Salwa Abdel-Aziz
Jane Allan & Mark Redmond
Lorraine Baker & Peter Hunkin
H & B Bamford
Lawrence Bartak
Jenny Blencowe
Fay Bock
Janet Brasch
Marianne & Robert Broadbent
Dr Christopher & Jill Buckley
Robyn Burke & Graham Burke AO
Anthony & Jan Burn
Elaine Chia & Ettore Altomare
Pamela Chin
Min Li Chong
Mr Peter R Clements
Kate Culbertson
Rosie Cunningham
David & Patricia Davidson
Beverley Davis OAM JP & Dr John Davis
Jenny & Nicholas Dawes
Ruth D
Mary Dyer
Isabel & Graeme Edgoose
Edith Gordon
Geoffrey Grinton OAM & Margaret Grinton
Sally Gudgeon
Katherine Horwood
Rachel & Peter Irons
Dr Michael & Pamela Jonas
Sarah Kimball
Julie Lidgett
Tabitha Lovett
C.N. Luth Esq.
Joy Manners
The Mar Family
Ann McLaren
Glenn & Maureen Monckton
Ruth Muir
Margaret Newton
Helen Oakes
Denis O'Hara & Annette Clarey
Tony Oliver
Dr Hannah Piterman
D Probert
Dr Amanda Reich
Ian Renard
Rock Posters
John Rogerson & Lynette Julian
Andrew Scott
Julie Shelton
Anthony Steward
Ronella Stuart
Diane Tweeddale
Fiona Viney
Sally Wallis
Dianne & Chris White
Richard Zimmermann
Anonymous (146)

Thank you

Melbourne Theatre Company would like to thank the following organisations for their generous support.

Major Partner

MinterEllison.

Future Directors Initiative Partner

Major Marketing Partner

The Monthly

The Saturday Paper

Associate Partners

Challis & Company — Tomorrow's leaders today

Frontier software — Human Capital Management & Payroll Software/Services

K&L GATES

THE LANGHAM MELBOURNE

SCOTCHMANS HILL — BELLARINE PENINSULA VICTORIA ESTABLISHED 1982

Supporting Partners

COMMUNE WINE

Genovese Coffee

invicium

The Luxury Network

METROPOLIS EVENTS

QUEST SOUTHBANK

southgate

Wilson Parking

Marketing Partners

Cinema Nova

RRR

Southbank Theatre Partner

mgc The Melbourne Gin Company

Business Collective Members

Committee for Melbourne

Leadership Collective Australia

Schuler Shook

Current as of September 2025.